MEDITATION

AND

SPIRITUAL

CONTEMPLATION

By

Terence McCarthy

Terence McCarthy

PublishAmerica

Second printing

PublishAmerica has allowed this work to remain exactly as the author intended, verbatim, without editorial input.

Hardcover 9781462609727
Softcover 9781462609710
PUBLISHED BY PUBLISHAMERICA, LLLP
www.publishamerica.com

ALSO BY TERENCE MCCARTHY

TITLE	PUBLISHER
COURTSHIP AND MARRIAGE (Shakesperian sonnet poems)	Dorrance & Company, Inc.
POETRY WITH FEELING (Shakesperian sonnet poems)	Publish America
ENJOYING LIFE AFTER 55 BY DOING THE RIGHT STUFF	Publish America
RUNNING UNTIL YOU ARE 100	Publish America

SECTION 1: INTRODUCTION

Life can be impossibly demanding. There are so many pies that we have our fingers in. Too often, we find that our achievements fall far short of our expectations. This can result in a scattered life style with huge fragmentations.

Computers also run into wide-spread, scattered situations which require time consuming searches on a frequent basis. To take care of this situation, we run a program called "defragmentation".

A similar situation develops in our own hectic life styles. The "defragmentation" program that we need to run is called "meditation".

Meditation comes from the Latin word "meditori" which means to heal.

Meditation is an extremely powerful process which can result in peace of mind and significant stress reduction.

The benefits are multi-dimensional. Studies have shown major improvements in the following areas: emotional, mental, physical and spiritual.

The key thing to remember is that the meditation process needs to be strictly followed in a completely effortless manner.

This is not a process for control freaks or micro-managers. Leave all of these willful inclinations behind as well as connections to the material world and just observe the program guidelines. If you approach the meditation process with this in mind, you will be pleasantly amazed at the results.

From my own personal experience in using meditation for nearly forty years, I have found each meditation event very refreshing and rewarding.

In the beginning I was totally unaware of any changes in myself. In this regard, the effects of meditation are very subtle and seemingly unproductive. The "desert" experiences are quite common where you observe mostly "dry" and "cold" emotions.

After six to seven weeks of daily meditating, people started commenting about how my behavior had changed in that I appeared happier and always seemed to be smiling.

Everyone is quite unique. There is no set standard for what you should or should not experience. The important thing is to closely follow the process guidelines and you will eventually find that the program works in spite of yourself.

What can you expect if you practice meditation on a daily basis? On an intellectual plane, it is one of the only times in our lives where we can leave self behind and where we are not materially involved. We become free from distractions and personal worries. We arrive at a higher state of consciousness which is profoundly restful. This leads to an overall sense of well being.

Finally, meditation is a prime example of the unity of mind and body. Mental stress can speed the heart up and raise blood pressure. Mediation can actually reverse this condition. Scientific studies demonstrate that meditation can slow the heart rate, lower blood pressure, reduce the breathing rate, diminish the body's oxygen consumption and reduce blood adrenaline levels.

SECTION 2: BASIC MEDITATION

Meditation is best performed in a quiet, semi-darkened place or in an environment where there is a constant, low level noise such as a fan. You can meditate indoors or outdoors. You should avoid areas which have loud noises or have intermittent noise disturbances.

Normally, it is important to sit with an erect posture with your eyes closed. If there is a bright light source in the area, wear a mask over your eyes to insure your sense of "darkness" and privacy. Breathe slowly and deeply. Allow your mind to become aware of your breathing rhythms

Next, you should start internally saying your mantra. Continue to say your mantra throughout the entire meditation. What is a "mantra". During the meditation process it is important that you use a "mantra" as the catalyst in achieving your departure from the self and ascending to a higher state of consciousness. The "mantra" should be a monosyllabic or a dual syllabic word such as "one" or "seven"

For the meditation to work, you need to repeat the mantra internally during the entire meditation period. This is the only willful act on your part during the meditation process.

It is recommended that you meditate for twenty minutes twice each day. The times of day that are best to meditate are in the morning before breakfast and later in the day before the evening meal. Never meditate after eating a meal since the deep state of rest that you might achieve, can interfere with the digestive process. The length and times of meditation are up to you. In the beginning it is quite a challenge to sit still in an effortless and quiet manner for twenty minutes. Having regularly scheduled meditation events on each day will increase the effectiveness and the benefits of the process.

So now you are in the meditation process and you are faithfully repeating your mantra in an effortless manner. But, there is a problem—your thoughts keep interrupting the process. In the beginning this is quite common and normal. These thoughts will normally be connected with your daily activities, worries and stress. Allow them to take over the scene for thirty seconds or more. Then, sweep them away by repeating your mantra. During your first several weeks of meditating, this annoying interference can be quite frequent. Don't despair, this is called the stress reduction part of the process. On many occasions you feel quite refreshed after the meditation.

What is the goal of the meditation process? The goal is to detach yourself from the distractions and the involvement in the material world and to reach a level in the process where there is absolutely nothing. This latter experience is your entry into a higher state of consciousness which is enormously beneficial.

By following the golden rule of constantly repeating the mantra, you can effectively suppress all thoughts. This ultimately leads to silence, nothingness and greater awareness.

The absolute necessity of repeating the mantra throughout the entire meditation process cannot be overemphasized. The mantra is articulated internally in your mind. It becomes rooted in your heart. You continue saying it no matter what. This is instrumental in avoiding the "pernicious peace" which occurs when you stop saying the mantra and drift off to sleep. Fortunately, saying the mantra is a purely mechanical function which requires no special talent.

This concludes the commentary on the basic meditation process. Effortlessly, follow theses guidelines exactly and with perseverance. This will allow you to enjoy meditation and the many benefits that are generated in the process.

SECTION 3: SPIRITUAL CONTEMPLATION

Spiritual contemplation, an expanded form of meditation, is a work of grace. It involves adapting oneself to the objective reality of the Truth. This adaptation is achieved by the work of one's highest spiritual faculties—intelligence and will. It demands expression by the whole being in that it is living in harmony with the True order of things. The Truth man needs is not an abstraction but God himself. The paradox of spiritual contemplation is that God is never really known unless He is loved. One cannot love Him unless he does His will.

The teaching of Jesus Christ is the seed of a new life. Reception of His word by faith initiates man's transformation. It elevates him above this world and his own natural thoughts and desires. It transports him to a supernatural level. He discovers that Christ is living in him. From that moment forward, the door of eternity stands open in the depths of his soul. He is capable of exploring this new dimension in spiritual contemplation.

Now that you understand the concept and the substance of spiritual contemplation, how do you go about obtaining the ascent to the supernatural level?

You need to divorce yourself from all of external sensory attractions that surround you. Then, you must place emphasis on your spiritual poverty and your object nothingness in the eyes of God.

You look at initiating the steps of basic meditation. There needs to be a quiet place with no noisy interruptions. You should have a good sitting posture. You need to discover and use a single or double syllabic word for your mantra. This should be of a spiritual nature such as: "Jesus" or "Spirit".

You continue to internally say the mantra throughout the contemplation. Your way is the way of silence. Silence is the way of the mantra. You are not talking to God. You are doing nothing but listening to His words. As St. John of the Cross constantly stated: "Silence is the basis for prayer not our discursiveness". By turning the focus of emphasis away from the self, this gives you a deeper awareness of God. By persevering in repeating the mantra, you are led to your dependence on Another.

It can be said that the aim of spiritual contemplation is to awaken the Holy Spirit within you and to bring your heart into harmony with His voice. This allows the Holy Spirit to speak and pray within you, raising the level of consciousness of His prayers in your heart.

Spiritual contemplation does not have to be spectacular or sensational. Its fruits are harvested in the depths of the soul, in the will and intelligence—not in the level of emotions. The fact that the contemplation appears "dry" or "cold", may be a sign providing great strength and raising your interior life above the senses.

Since it is impossible for the human mind to have a clear and comprehensive understanding of the things of God, the contemplative experience of divine things is achieved in the darkness of faith which is surrounded by a vast indefiniteness. Thus, the function of contemplation is to bring you in some way into the conscious communion with God who is the source of natural and supernatural life.

Contemplation is spiritual and difficult. It requires sincerity, humility and perseverance. These are reinforced by the awakening of your interior self and attuning yourself inwardly to the Holy Spirit. This leads to the abandonment to the will and action of God. Attaining this conformity to God's will results in your being rewarded with grace and staying power in your spiritual life.

On a personal note, when I start my spiritual contemplation, I go through the following routine. I say " Praise you and thank you Jesus. Jesus Christ is Lord. Jesus be with me". Then, I start saying my mantra. This puts me at a higher level and opens the door to invite Jesus into my contemplation. By saying the words: "Jesus Christ is Lord" we are invoking Paul's advice to us in 1 Corinthians 12 where he states: " No one can confess Jesus is Lord, unless he is guided by the Holy Spirit". This assures us that we are indeed in a state of grace and accompanied by the Holy Spirit.

SECTION 4: MYSTICAL CONTEMPLATION

After experiencing the initial contemplation process, we are ready to move into a more profound relationship with God. This is called mystical contemplation which is a free supernatural gift of God.

Mystical contemplation is a vivid, conscious participation of our soul in life, knowledge and love of God. Love is the cornerstone of this experience. Without love of God and thanksgiving for His gift, we can never fully participate in mystical contemplation.

This experience is directly caused by special inspirations of the Holy Spirit substantially present in the soul itself. Above all this gives us a deep penetration into the truth of our identification with God by grace.

Since the act of faith is the first step toward contemplation, it is important to know what faith is. Faith is a supernatural virtue which enables the intelligence of man to make a firm commitment to divinely revealed truths. The object of faith is God Himself. This is reinforced by St. John of the Cross who has stated that "faith alone is the proximate and proportional means by which the soul is united to God."

It is significant to note St. John of the Cross's view of contemplation. He maintains that contemplation obscures the clear knowledge of divine things and that it hides them in a "cloud of unknowing". In this "cloud", God communicates to the soul passively and in darkness. Three clear statements by St. John of the Cross show the exact function of the "unknowing":

1. Acquired knowledge of God should not be discarded as long as it helps man toward Divine Union.

2. Concepts that interfere with the "obscure" mystical illuminations of the soul should be rejected.

3. Do not renounce the desire of clear, conceptual knowledge of God unless you are receiving infused prayer (a gift of God).

Special inspirations of the Holy Spirit can never be merited by us or acquired. These are supernatural gifts that reason must dispose itself for reception.

A few souls let the gifts of God fall out of their hands by inactivity or wasting efforts on the wrong thing. The most common fault is that too many contemplatives remain tangled up in externals or in concrete, limiting concepts.

The secret of progress in the interior life (mystical contemplation) is to escape from ourselves as quickly and as completely as possible and give ourselves entirely to God.

Thomas Merton sums up mystical contemplation as follows:

"the highest spiritual good is an action which is so perfect that it is absolutely free of all labor, and is therefore at the same time perfect action and rest. And, this is the contemplation of God."

SECTION 5: LISTENING TO THE VOICE OF THE LORD

In the Spiritual Contemplation, you are focused on listening to the voice of the Lord. How are you going to go about this and have some assurance that you are listening to His voice and not yours? It is suggested that prior to your contemplation event, you may want to use the technique of "Listening To The Voice Of The Lord".

The following technique is one that has proven to be quite successful over the years. You should approach it with a certain degree of caution. Confirmation from another source should be obtained before proceeding to act on any answers received.

Receive the Lord in your heart. Ask for forgiveness for all of your sins. Forgive others who have wronged you.

Command Satan's voice "In the name of Jesus Christ who is Lord, I command Satan to be quiet. I also command my voice to be silent except for the purpose of talking to the Lord".

Ask the question:

"Are you the Jesus Christ who is Lord"?

The answer you should hear:

"Yes, I am the Jesus Christ who is Lord".

Upon receiving the full answer (not just "Yes, I am), you have verified that you are indeed hearing the voice of the Lord. Satan cannot interfere or answer in this situation. This procedure is authenticated by the words of St. Paul in the 1st letter to the Corinthians where he confirmed that if you can say "Jesus Christ is Lord, you are indeed filled with the Holy Spirit".

Then, ask: "What is it Lord that you want to tell me"? Listen.

Now that you have started your dialogue with the Lord, continue your conversation and ask Him questions as the Spirit guides you. Remember to pray over answers which direct you to act in a major way e.g. "change your job" or "give up everything and go live in Jerusalem". Pray to God for confirmation so that you can act with discernment.

St. Paul in Hebrews 4 issues two statements that we should bear in mind: "If you hear God's voice today, do not be stubborn".

"The word of God is alive, sharper than any double edged sword. It cuts all the way through to where soul and spirit meet."

SECTION 6: BENEFITS OF MEDITATION/SPIRITUAL CONTEMPLATION

Many studies have been conducted on the benefits of meditation. Since spiritual contemplation is an expanded form of meditation, it is included in the general category: "meditation" in this section.

The benefits are broken down into the following categories: Emotional, Mental, Physical and Spiritual. They are included in Sections 7, 8, 9 and 10.

Since each individual is different and will have a very personal and unique experience in the use of either meditation process described in this book, the benefits of meditation may vary markedly from one person to the next.

Suffice it to say, the observed benefits discussed in these studies may or may not apply in each personal situation.

SECTION 7: EMOTIONAL BENEFITS

- Become more stable

- Improve relationships

- Reduce depression

- Become more productive

- Reduce stress

- Help with personal grief

- Reduce anxiety attacks

- Increase well being

SECTION 8: MENTAL BENEFITS

- Increase creativity

- Improve memory

- Increase listening skills

- Become more motivated

- Increase discernment

- Fight mental aging

- Become more focused

- Strengthen will power

SECTION 9: PHYSICAL BENEFITS

- Reduce needs for sleep

- Reduce blood pressure

- Provide pain relief

- Reduce chronic diseases

- Fight degenerative diseases of aging

- Provide relief for headaches

- Increase life's longevity

- Relax nervous system

- Slow down heart rate

- Increase and aid circulation

- Lower cholesterol

SECTION 10: SPIRITUAL BENEFITS

- Expand consciousness

- Become more spiritual

- Aid in accepting your self

- Unite mind, body and spirit

- Increase capacity for love

- Provide inner peace

- Understand the self better

SECTION 11: SUMMARY

You now have the tools to develop a greater self-realization and achieve a much more profound sense of well being.

Like anything else in life, it is up to you to apply yourself and earn this new union of mind, body and spirit. This will require a major effort on your part. Maintain a zero level of expectations. Be patient and let the process do its own thing.

The one thing that you can be sure of is this: this is a tried and proven process that works as long as you allow it to proceed in an effortless and "hands off" manner.

NOTE: The recent copy of April 2011 Consumer Reports "On Health" stated that "studies show that meditating regularly can lower blood pressure and reduce the need for medication".

SECTION 12: AUTHOR COMMENTARY

I have been using the meditation technique since 1973. I started out when I spent some time in the French Alps with Maharishi Mahesh Yogi, the founder of the Transcendental Meditation movement.

Academically, I earned my masters degree from the University of Southern California in 1975. My masters thesis was on meditation which contains extensive scientific studies on the benefits of meditation. Some of these definitely show impacts on dementia and Alzheimer's disease.

My experience has been tempered by the writings of Thomas Merton, the Trappist monk, St. John of the Cross and St. Thomas Aquinas.

The basic mechanics of the meditation process also apply to the mystical contemplation experience. I strongly support the employment of a solid preparation process so that you can more effectively communicate with God as follows:

1. Enter into a short praise and thanksgiving to the Lord.
2. Verify your being is in the state of grace by using St. Paul's words: "Jesus Christ is Lord".
3. Invite the Lord into your heart with the simple words: "Jesus be with me".
4. Concentrate on the repetition of your mantra to keep yourself focused on God and to maintain a complete separation from your senses, worries and worldly distractions.
5. Re-visit the meditation process several times each day to re-inforce the mystical contemplation experience.

By doing some or all these steps, you are placing your soul in the "unknowing cloud" and creating the potential for the receipt of infused prayer. All of this is done outside of emotional and spectacular experiences. Our faith leads us to special inspirations which result in the Divine Union with God.